The Nature in Close-up Series

1 The Life of a Butterfly
3 Food Chains
4 Garden Spider
5 The Dragonfly
6 Honeybees
7 Insects we Need
8 Tree in a Wood
9 Moths
10 Owls
11 Life under Stones
12 Waterside Birds
13 Frogs and Toads
14 Wasps
15 Pond Life
16 Seabirds
17 Foxes
18 Town Birds
19 Beetles
20 Snakes

Martin, Graham R
Owls. – (Nature in close up ; 10).
1. Owls
I. Title II. Series
598.9'7 QL696.S8
ISBN 0-7136-2035-8

Acknowledgements

The photographs on pages 10, 12 and 13 (top left) are reproduced by permission of Ron Saunders and those on pages 14 and 15 (top right) by permission of Derick Scott. The remaining photographs are reproduced by permission of Aquila Photographics.

Published by A & C Black (Publishers) Limited
35 Bedford Row, London WC1R 4JH

First published 1980
© 1980 Graham R Martin
Reprinted 1983
All rights reserved. No part of this publication may be reproduced, stored in a retrieval system, or transmitted, in any form or by any means, electronic, mechanical, photocopying, recording or otherwise, without the prior permission of A & C Black (Publishers) Limited

Printed in Hong Kong by Dai Nippon Printing Co. Ltd

Nature in Close-up

OWLS

Graham R. Martin

Adam & Charles Black · London

Contents

Introduction 2
Birds of the night 4
Birds of prey 7
Eyes and ears to hunt with 8
Feathers and silent flight 10
Feet, legs and bills 12
Diet and pellets 14
Habitats and nests 16
Owlets 20
Some owl species 22
European species 24
North American species 25
Index 26

Introduction

Owls are very easy to recognise. They have flat faces with large, forward-facing eyes, hooked bills and needle-sharp talons on their feet.

Owls are birds of prey. This means they live by capturing and eating other small animals, including birds.

You don't often see owls, but you can sometimes hear them. Most are nocturnal, hunting at night and hiding away during the day. They make hooting, shrieking and hissing calls throughout the night.

There are 135 species of owls, found in all parts of the world. The Snowy Owl lives in the cold wastes of the Arctic tundra; the hot, humid jungles of the Equator are the home of the Fishing Owl.

Owls range in size from the Elf Owl (14cm long) to the Eagle Owl, which is over 70cm long and has a wing span of about 150cm.

A Tawny Owl

Birds of the night

During the day, most owls are roosting. If you look very carefully, you may find one inside a hollow tree, or a farm building, or sitting on a branch near the tree trunk. It will seem to be dozing, but nobody knows whether owls actually sleep in the way that we do.

When owls are roosting, they don't often move, so they are difficult to see. Also, they have brown and grey feathers on their wings, back and tail, which help to camouflage them when they are sitting with their wings folded.

Some owls leave their roost at dusk. Others don't venture out until well after dark. They return to their roost at dawn.

This Little Owl has waited until well after dark to emerge from his roost ▶

These Barn Owls look as though they have been disturbed at their roost ▼

Birds of prey

The creatures that an owl hunts are called its prey. An owl kills its prey and then usually swallows it whole.

There are two different ways in which owls hunt. Some owls use the 'perch and pounce' method. They sit on a perch for long periods, silent and still. When the prey comes close, they capture it in a single pounce.

Other owls fly slowly up and down, just above a field, and pounce when a small animal passes by below. This way of hunting is called 'quartering'.

◀ A Barn Owl flying with its prey in its bill

▲ A Tawny Owl about to eat a House Sparrow

Eyes and ears to hunt with

The eyes of owls are very large. They are not much more sensitive than our eyes, but at night owls can see some things which we can't.

Owls don't have large visible parts to their ears as we do, but the actual openings are bigger than ours. They are underneath the feathers at the edge of the face. In the picture of a Barn Owl below, you can see the clear line round the edge of its face.

▲ A Little Owl. Its eyes are large, with yellow irises (coloured part of the eye)

◀ Face of a Barn Owl

Owls can't move their ears in the way that other animals can. Also, their eyes are so large that they can't move them in their sockets. Because of this, owls have developed very flexible necks. They can look directly behind them (like the Tawny Owl in this picture) and can even turn their heads almost upside down.

Feathers and silent flight

The wing feathers have tiny comb-like teeth on their front edges. Using these, owls can fly without making any noise.

Owls often have to sit still in the open for many hours waiting for prey. Those which live where there are long winter nights have a lot of very soft downy feathers. These protect them from the bitter cold.

Owls even have feathers on their eyelids and down their legs to the tips of their toes. They also have soft hairs on their wings and tail feathers, which give extra warmth.

▲ Soft downy feathers. These protect owls from the bitter cold.

A Barn Owl in flight ▶

Feet, legs and bills

The feet, legs and bills of owls are especially adapted for catching prey.

An owl's legs are very thick and strong, so that it can grip its prey tightly in its talons. The feet are large and the talons are very sharp. An owl pounces with its talons spread out. When the owl hits its victim, it closes its talons tightly around it. Small mice and birds are often killed simply by the shock of the impact.

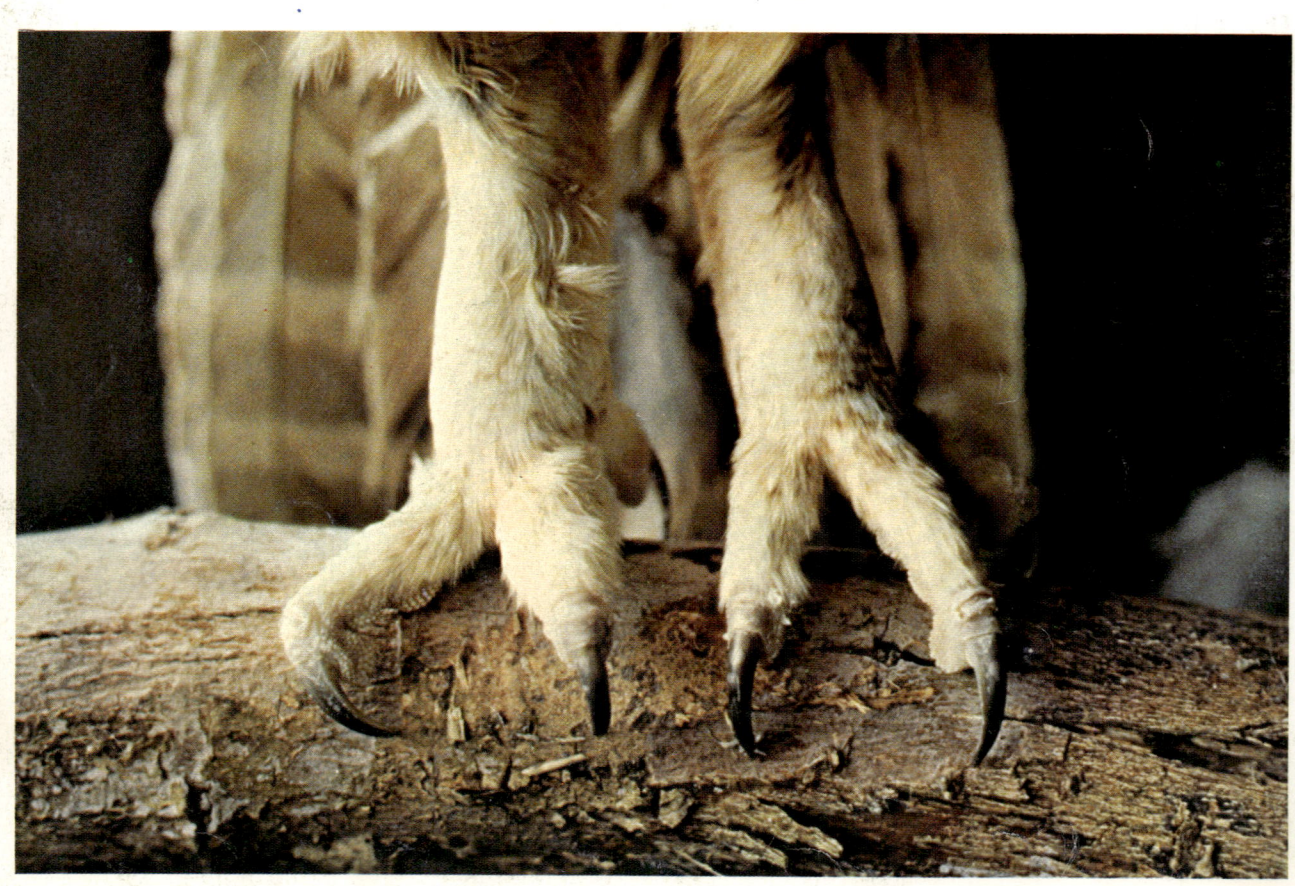

The bill is sharply hooked. If the prey is too large to be eaten whole, the owl tears it up with its bill. Owls have large mouths so they can swallow their prey in big pieces.

A Barn Owl holding its prey in its bill ▶

Diet and pellets

The food owls eat is usually very varied. Their diet may include earthworms, insects, small birds, rats, voles and mice. Some owl species from the tropics even eat fish.

All owls help us because they eat pests. This is one reason why owls are specially protected by law.

Owls cannot digest certain parts of their prey, like bones, fur and feathers, or the hard wing cases of beetles. They empty their stomachs of these parts by 'regurgitating' (bringing up and spitting out) pellets. Sometimes you can find owl pellets on the ground.

▲ Pellets of different owl species are different sizes and shapes

◀ Finding an owl pellet

You can soak a pellet in a saucer of water and then take it apart with tweezers. You will see the bones of the animals the owl has eaten. Jaw bones and teeth are the easiest to recognise. This is a good way of finding out what different kinds of owls eat.

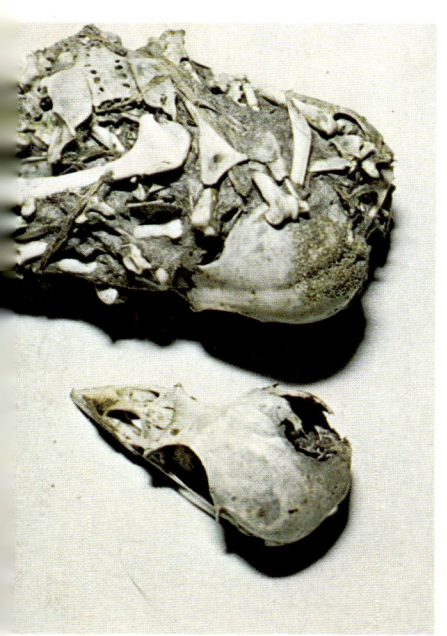

Contents of an owl pellet which has been dissected ▼

▲ Children dissecting an owl pellet

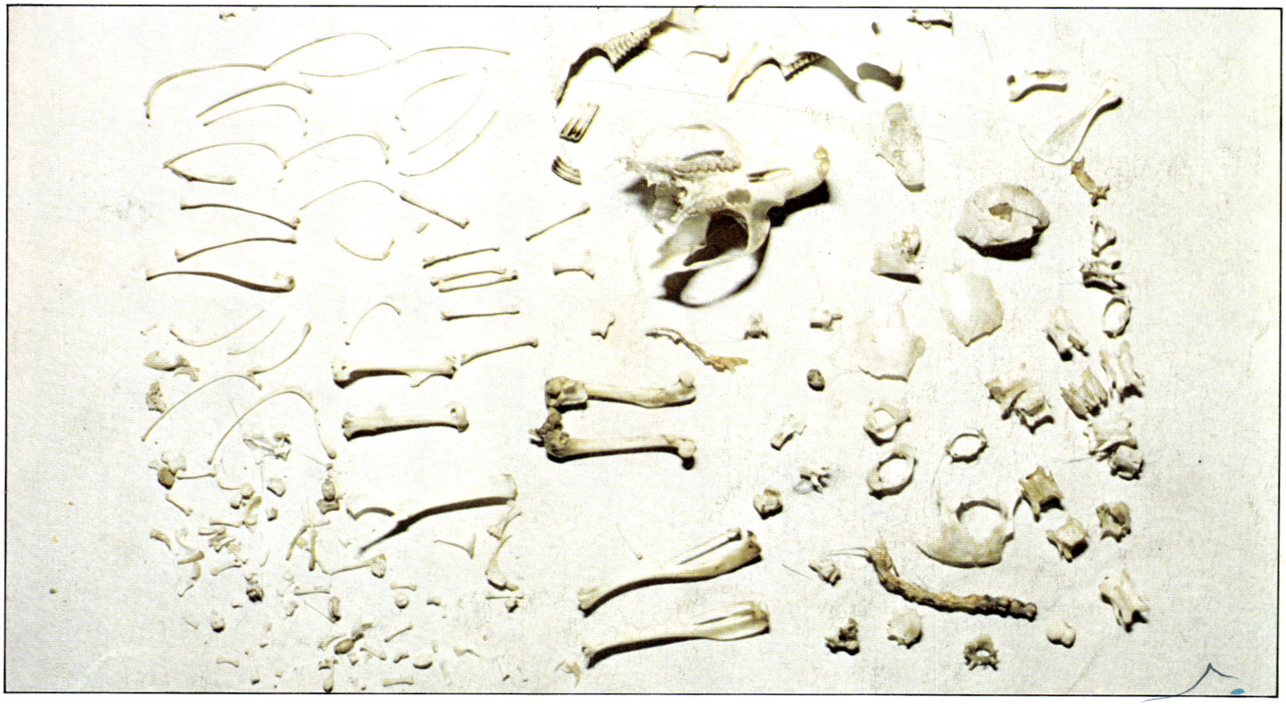

Habitats and nests

In Europe and North America, owls can be found living and breeding in nearly every kind of habitat. The nests are always very simple. Owls often use the old nests of other birds such as magpies and crows.

The Short-Eared Owl, like the one in the picture below, lives in open grassland areas. Its nest is just a hollow in the ground.

Opposite is a photograph of the nest of a Long-Eared Owl. It's an old crow's nest, and is made of twigs. The Long-Eared Owl prefers living in dark conifer woods.

Barn Owls live on or near farms. Farmers like them because they catch rats and mice, which eat corn and other stored foods. Barn Owls make their nests on ledges high up inside barns, as in the photograph above.

Little Owls usually make their nests inside hollow trees. Occasionally, they use a hole in a wall. The entrance to the Little Owl's nest in the photograph opposite is less than a metre from the ground.

Many owls will breed in nest boxes. By using specially designed nest boxes, the Tawny Owl, Little Owl and Barn Owl have all been successfully encouraged to breed in places where natural nest sites were not available.

Owlets

Young owls are called owlets. When they hatch, they are covered in soft downy feathers. Their parents bring food back to the nest, tear it up and feed it to their young. Sometimes owlets tear up food for themselves.

In Europe and North America, owls lay their eggs in March or early April. The eggs take about one month to hatch. The owlets grow very quickly, but their adult feathers take four or five months to develop.

Little Owlets ▼

Owlets often leave their nest well before they can fly. They walk around near the nest calling to their parents for food.

It usually takes many months before the owlets learn to hunt on their own. Their parents go on feeding them all this time.

Tawny Owlets ▼

Some owl species

The various species of owls divide into two families – the Barn Owl family and the Typical Owl family.

The Barn Owls have beautiful, heart-shaped faces. Their fronts and the undersides of their wings are often pure white. There are eleven species and their scientific family name is *Tytonidae*. Only one species of *Tytonidae* lives in Europe and North America. This is the Common Barn Owl.

The Typical Owls have more rounded faces. They are usually brown or grey underneath. There are 124 species in the world and their scientific family name is *Strigidae*.

The owl species shown on these two pages live both in Europe and North America. The species on page 24 live only in Europe, and those on page 25 only in North America.

▲ Snowy Owl

Short-Eared Owl ▶

Long-Eared Owl ▶

European species

The Tawny Owl and the Little Owl are the commonest owls in Europe. The Tawny Owl prefers to live in woodland. The Little Owl likes open parkland and farms.

The Eagle Owl is the largest of all owls. It lives in remote forests among mountain ranges.

Little Owl ▶

▼ Tawny Owl

▼ Eagle Owl

North American species

The Great Horned Owl is the most common owl in North America. It is large and has a wing span of 140cm. It lives in woods and open country.

The Barred Owl lives in woods and prefers areas close to swamps and river valleys.

The Saw Whet Owl gets its name from its peculiar call. It is a small owl and lives in evergreen woods.

▲ Great Horned Owl

▼ Saw Whet Owl

▼ Barred Owl

Index

Barn Owl *4, 6, 8, 11, 13,* 18, 22
Barred Owl 25, *25*

Eagle Owl *2, 24,* 24
ears 9
Elf Owl 2
eyes 8

feathers 10
Fishing Owl 2

Great Horned Owl 25, *25*

legs 12
Little Owl *5, 8,* 18, *20, 24,* 24
Long-Eared Owl *17, 23*

nests 16

owlets 20–21

pellets 14, *15*
'perch and pounce' 7
prey 2, 7

'quartering' 7

roosting 4

Saw Whet Owl 25, *25*
Short-Eared Owl 16, *16,* 22
Snowy Owl 2, 22, *22*
Strigidae 22

talons 12
Tawny Owl *3, 7, 9, 9,* 18, *21,* 22, *24,* 24
Tytonidae 22